AARON JAY KERNIS

SIMPLE SONGS

FOR SOPRANO AND PIANO

AMP 8233
First Printing: July 2008

ISBN: 978-1-4234-5871-5

Associated Music Publishers, Inc.

DISTRIBUTED BY
HAL•LEONARD®
CORPORATION
7777 W. BLUEMOUND RD. P.O. BOX 13819 MILWAUKEE, WI 53213

SIMPLE SONGS

I

Holy Spirit,
giving life to all life,
moving all creatures,
root of all things,
washing them clean,
wiping out their mistakes,
healing their wounds,
you are our true life,
luminous, wonderful,
awakening the heart
from its ancient sleep.

—Hildegard of Bingen (1098–1179)

II

Blessed are the man and the woman
        who have grown beyond their greed
        and have put an end to their hatred
        and no longer nourish illusions.
But they delight in the way things are
        and keep their hearts open, day and night.
They are like trees planted near flowing rivers,
        which bear fruit when they are ready.
Their leaves will not fall or wither.
        Everything they do will succeed.

—Psalm 1

Texts from *The Enlightened Heart,* Copyright © 1989 Stephen Mitchell, published 1989 by Harper & Row, New York.
Used with generous permission of Stephen Mitchell. Translation of Rumi *"You are the notes, and we are the flute,"*
Copyright © 1983 Robert Bly, used by permission by George Borchardt, Inc.

III

First days of spring—the sky
is bright blue, the sun huge and warm.
Everything's turning green.
Carrying my monk's bowl, I walk to the village
to beg for my daily meal.
The children spot me at the temple gate
and happily crowd around,
dragging at my arms till I stop.
I put my bowl on a white rock,
hang my bag on a branch.
First we braid grasses and play tug-of-war,
then we take turns singing and keeping a kick-ball in the air:
I kick the ball and they sing, they kick and I sing.
Time is forgotten, the hours fly.
People passing by point at me and laugh:
"Why are you acting like such a fool?"
I nod my head and don't answer.
I could say something, but why?
Do you want to know what is in my heart?
From the beginning of time: just this! just this!

—Ryokan (1758–1831)

IV

You are the notes, and we are the flute.
We are the mountain, you are the sounds coming down.
We are the pawns and kings and rooks
you set out on a board: we win or we lose.
We are the lions rolling and unrolling on flags.
Your invisible wind carries us through the world.

—Rumi (1207–1273)

V

Lord, my mind is not noisy with desires,
        and my heart has satisfied its longing.
I do not care about religion
        or anything that is not you.
I have soothed and quieted my soul,
        like a child at its mother's breast.
My soul is as peaceful as a child
        sleeping in its mother's arms.

—Psalm 131

SIMPLE SONGS *was commissioned by the Mary Flagler Cary Charitable Trust
for the New Music Consort, Claire Heldrich and Madeleine Shapiro, directors
and soprano Susan Narucki*

*The Chamber Orchestra Version was made with the assistance
of the Saint Paul Chamber Orchestra.*

A recording of SIMPLE SONGS *(soprano and chamber ensemble)
is available on Koch International Classics; KIC-CD-7667
with Susan Narucki, soprano and members of the New York Philharmonic Orchestra,
conducted by the composer.*

duration ca. 20 minutes

Available on rental from the Publisher

SIMPLE SONGS for Soprano and Chamber Ensemble
scored for Flute (Piccolo), Oboe, Horn in F, Percussion, Harp, String Quintet (2 Vns., Va., Vc., Cb.)

SIMPLE SONGS for Soprano and Chamber Orchestra
scored for Flute (Piccolo), Oboe, Horn in F, Percussion, Harp, Strings (minimum 6.6.4.4.2 players)

G. Schirmer and Associated Music Publishers Rental Department
P.O. Box 572
445 Bellvale Road
Chester, NY 10918
(845) 469-4699
(845) 469-7544 (fax)

Composer's Note

Simple Songs was composed in 1991 for Susan Narucki and the New Music Consort then expanded in 1995 for the St. Paul Chamber Orchestra. The work was initially commissioned by the Mary Flagler Cary Charitable Trust. This piano-vocal version was completed in 1998.

The texts come from *The Enlightened Heart*, an anthology of spiritual poetry from many countries and disciplines by Stephen Mitchell. Texts include two Psalms and one poem each by Christian mystic and composer Hildegard of Bingen (1098-1179), the Sufi poet Rumi (1207-1273), and the Buddhist monk, Ryokan (1758-1831). The fifth and final movement is dedicated to the memory of Leonard Bernstein.

—Aaron Jay Kernis

Information on Aaron Jay Kernis and his works is available at www.schirmer.com

SIMPLE SONGS

Hildegard of Bingen

Aaron Jay Kernis

I

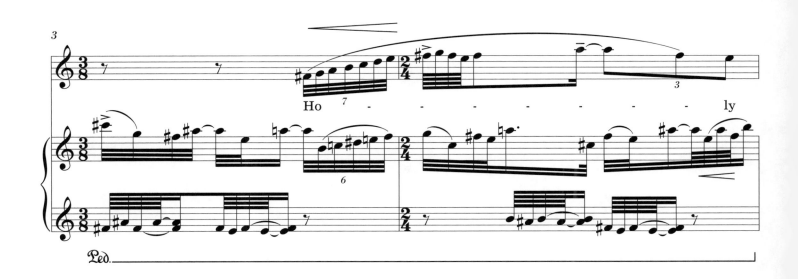

Spir-it, _____ giv - ing life to all

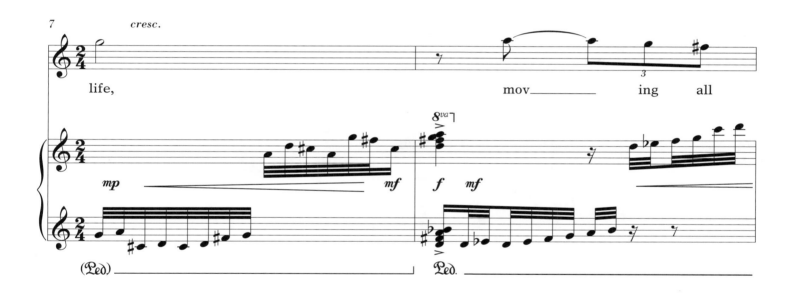

life, mov _____ ing all

crea - tures, root _____ of all things, _____

Tempo I

11 ♪ =100, ♩ = 50

wash-ing them_____ clean,

13

wip-ing out their mis - takes,

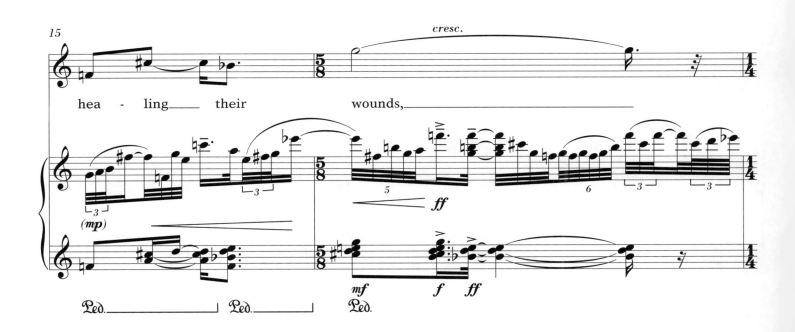

15

hea - ling_____ their wounds,_____

5

you are our true life, you are our true life,

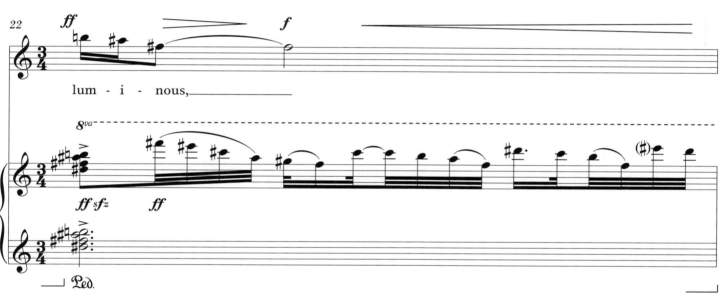

lum - i - nous,____

won - - der - - ful,

6

a - wak - e -ning the heart   from its an - cient

sleep.

attacca

Psalm 1

Bles - - - sed_ are the man_ and the wo-man_

who have grown be-yond their greed and have put_ an end_ to their

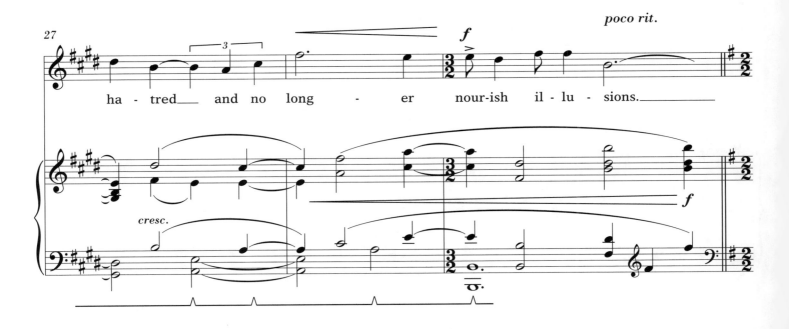

ha - tred_ and no long - er nour-ish il - lu - sions._

But they de - light in the way things are

and keep their hearts o - pen, day and night.

They are like trees plan-ted

near flow - ing ri - vers,___ which_ bear

fruit___ when they are rea-dy.___

Their leaves will not fall or wi - ther. Ev - 'ry

thing they do will suc - ceed.

Ryokan

III

First__ days of spring– the sky__ __ is bright blue, the sun__ huge__ and warm. Eve-ry-thing's turn-ing green.__

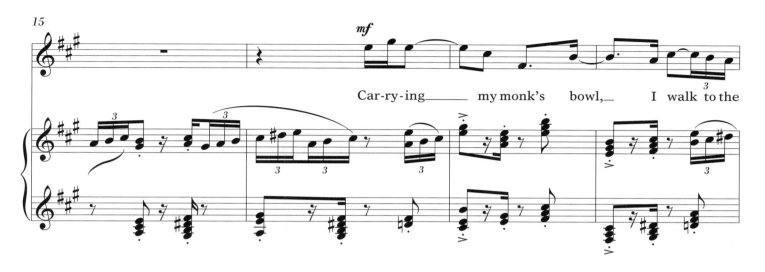

Car-ry-ing _____ my monk's bowl, _____ I walk to the

vil - lage _____ to beg _____ for my dai - ly meal. _____

The child-ren spot me _ at the tem -ple gate and hap - pi-ly crowd _

__'round, drag - ging_ at my arms___ 'til I stop._

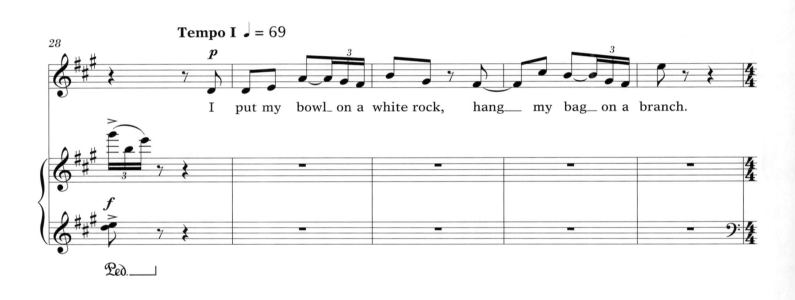

I put my bowl_ on a white rock, hang_ my bag_ on a branch.

First_ we braid gras - ses_

and play tug-of-war,

then we take turns sing- ing and keep-ing a kick-ball in the air:

I kick the ball and they sing, they kick and I sing.

Time⸺⸺⸺⸺⸺⸺ is for - got - ten,

the hou - - - rs fly.⸺⸺⸺⸺⸺

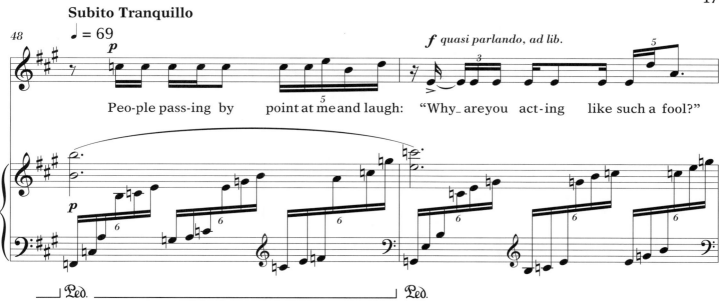

Peo-ple pass-ing by point at me and laugh: "Why_ are you act-ing like such a fool?"

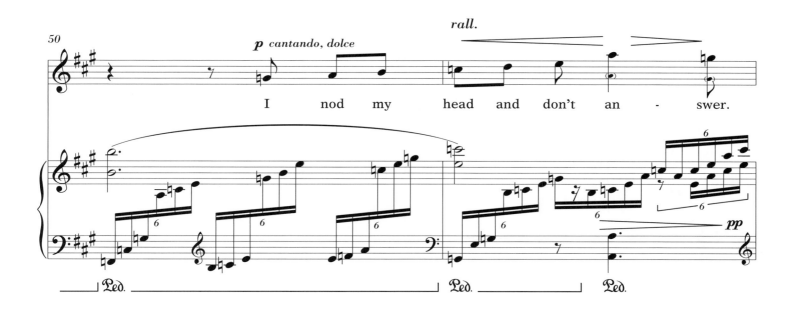

I nod my head and don't an - swer.

I should say some - thing, but why?_____

Do you want to know what's in my heart?

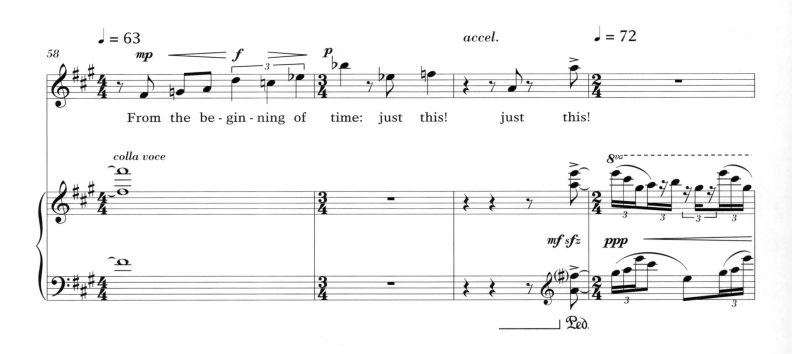

From the be-gin-ning of time: just this! just this!

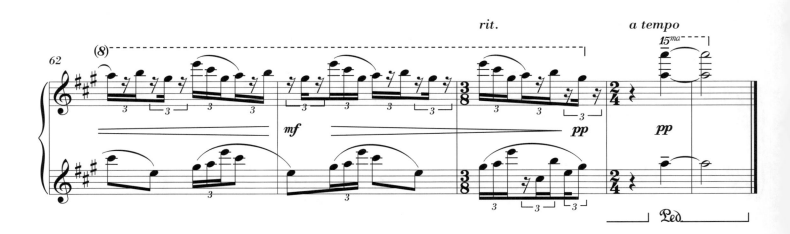

IV

Sostenuto ♩ = 38

You_____ are the notes and

we_____ are the flute._____

(Ped)

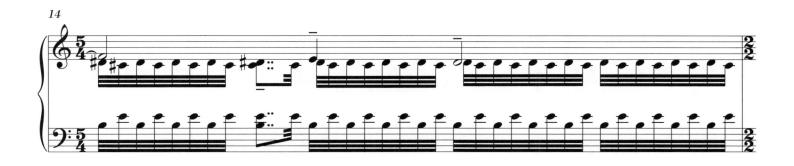

(Ped.) ⋀ *sempre*

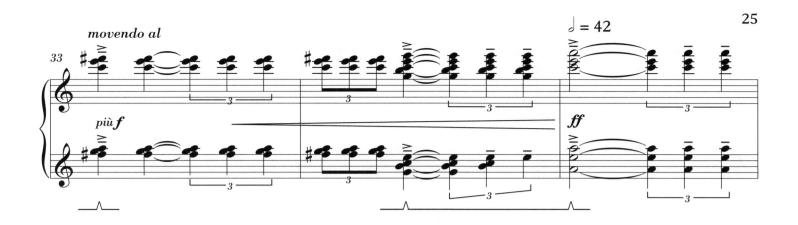

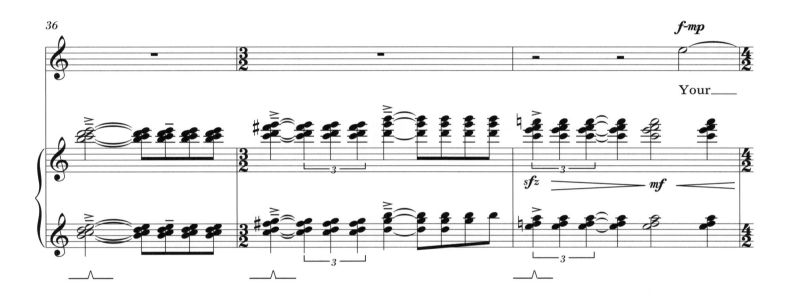

Your____

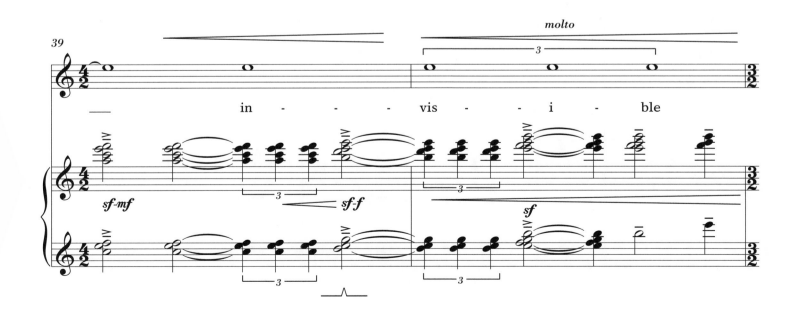

in - - vis - i - ble

Sostenuto ♩ = 40

wind_____ car - ries us_____ through_____ the_____ world.__

wind_____ car - ries us_____ through_____ the_____ world.__

accel. poco a poco

in memory of Leonard Bernstein

V

Lord,_____ Lord,_____ Lord,__

Pochiss. Più ♩ = 69
tranquillo

_____ my mind is not nois - y____ with de -

sires,_____ and my heart has sat - is - fied its

long - ing._____ I do not care__ a - bout re - lig - ion or

an - y - thing___ that is not you.___

I have soothed and qui - e - ted my soul,___

like a child___ at its moth-er's breast.___

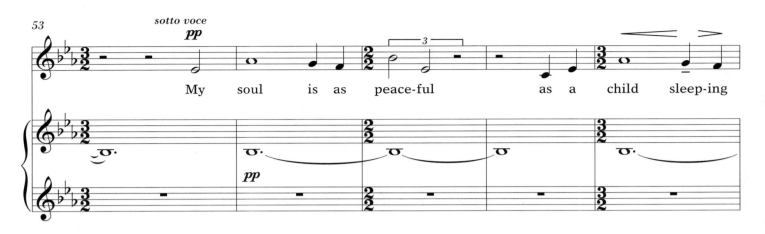

My soul is as peace-ful as a child sleep-ing

Tempo I ♩ = 60

in its mo - ther's arms.

(in relief)

(con Ped.)

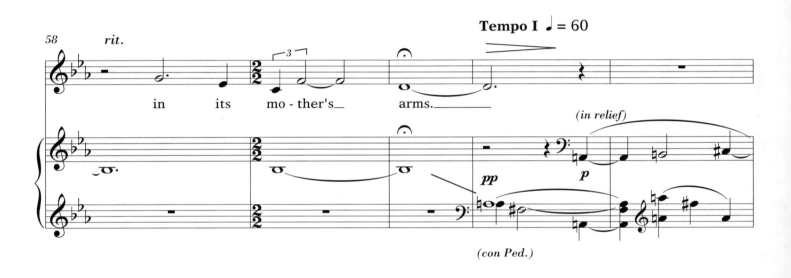

*: The soprano line from measure 80 through the end is optional when sung with piano accompaniment.
   It is never to be sung when performed in either ensemble version.